1|4|13
$14.95
QB
AS

D1530933

THE KID IN THE CRIB

THE KID IN THE CRIB

A
DR. SEUSS
PARODY

By Lex Friedman

ILLUSTRATED BY FELIX SCHLATER

LYONS PRESS
Guilford, Connecticut
An imprint of Globe Pequot Press

Lyons Press is an imprint of Globe Pequot Press.

Library of Congress Cataloging-in-Publication Data

Friedman, Lex.
 The kid in the crib : a Dr. Seuss parody / Lex Friedman ;
illustrations by Felix Jason Schlater.
     p. cm.
 Summary: "This delightful reimagining of the beloved children's book
The Cat in the Hat pays tribute to Dr. Seuss while lampooning his style
and narrative in a way that will leave beleagured parents giggling like,
well, children"— Provided by publisher.
 ISBN 978-0-7627-8304-5 (hardback)
 1. Seuss, Dr. Cat in the hat.—Parodies, imitations, etc. I. Title.
 PS3606.R565K53 2012
 813'.6—dc23
                                                        2012018704

Printed in the United States of America

10 9 8 7 6 5 4 3 2 1

To Anya, Sierra, and Liam—three kids worth waking up for
at all hours of the night. Now go back to sleep
until at least 6:00 a.m.

And to Lauren, for co-creating those
three wonderful children.

Her cries did not stop.
She was too mad to snore.
She spat up in the crib,
She spat up on the floor.

We tried to console her,
We tried to, we two.
And we said, "How we wish
We had half of a clue!"

The kid wouldn't sleep.
The kid wouldn't nurse.
Our cute little blessing
Was more of a curse.

So all we could say was just
Hush!
Hush!
Hush!
Hush!

And was it effective?
Well, not at first blush.

Fart!

And then something went FART!
That fart gave us a start!

We looked,
And we realized it had been the kid.
We turned
And concluded what
Baby just did.

And we said to each other,
"It's your turn this time."
She said, "I did the last one!"
But mine had more slime!

"I know what to do,"
I said in a soft whisper.
"Loser must change her—
Quick: rock, paper, scissors!"

My wife threw out paper,
And I threw out rock,
And I said, "The rules
Of this game are a crock."

A rock versus paper?
How could paper win?
No matter. "You lost,"
My wife said with a grin.

I scooped up the baby;
She cried and she cried,
As if we'd declared
That her Grandma just died.

I set down the baby
And checked my supplies;
I opened the diaper
And tuned out her cries.

And then I said, "No! No!
What has happened in there?!
Did you nurse her? Or feed her
Fresh meat from a bear?"
That poop was not human,
That poop seemed so phony,
That poop looked like
Mustard and tar and baloney.

"Now! Now! Have no fear,
Have no fear," said my wife.
"Her poop won't stay gross
Throughout all of her life."

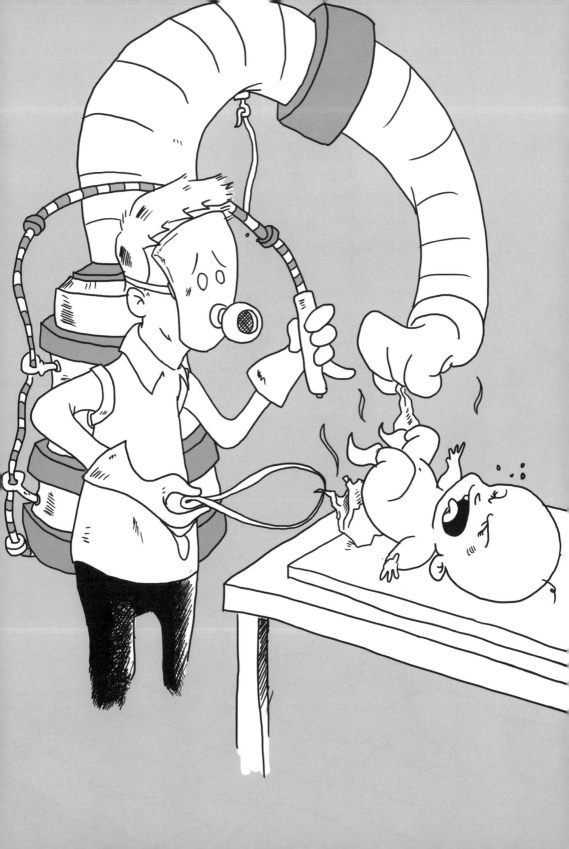

I disagreed,
But just nodded a "Yes."
I wanted to change her
Without a big mess.

The baby was writhing
As I held my breath
And wiped away smells
Of wet dog hair and death.

"Put it on!" said my wife.
"You are going too slow!
Put it on," said my wife,
"I think she's gonna blow!"

I wished that our baby
Could use the commode.
And I whispered a prayer:
"Please, oh please, don't explode."

As I fastened the diaper,
My wife slowly sat up.
And that's about when
Our dear baby spat up.

"Look at this!
Look at this stuff," I cried out.
"Call an exorcist!" my wife
Replied with a shout.

The kid spat up white,
The kid spat up green,
The kid spat up more spit-up
Than we'd ever seen.

She spat up on the table,
She spat up on the wall,
She spat up on my T-shirt,
And started to bawl.
But that was not all,
Oh, no,
That was not all.

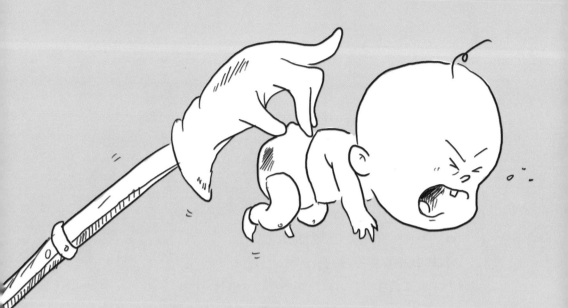

After a moment,
She stopped all her shrieking.
But then my wife said,
"Dear, I think that she's leaking!

Her diaper's distended,
Her diaper looks mushy,
And it's sure not containing
What's come from her tushy!"

Now I had just changed her,
Had *just* wiped her rear.
So I said to the missus,
"It's your turn now, dear."

My wife didn't speak,
She just gave me a glare.
Or perhaps you might call it
Her Evil Death Stare.

But slowly she stood
While I smiled quite brightly.
And softly she said,
"I'll put this one on *rightly*."

So she changed the baby—
She changed Baby quick—
And when she was finished,
Baby *didn't* get sick.

But did Baby stop crying?
No, Baby did not.
Baby's head spewed both tears
And some gushers of snot.

"I'll take her downstairs,"
I cried over her roaring.
Six seconds later,
My wife resumed snoring.

And Baby and I
Went downstairs to calm her—
Her wails could drown out
A dang F-18 Bomber.

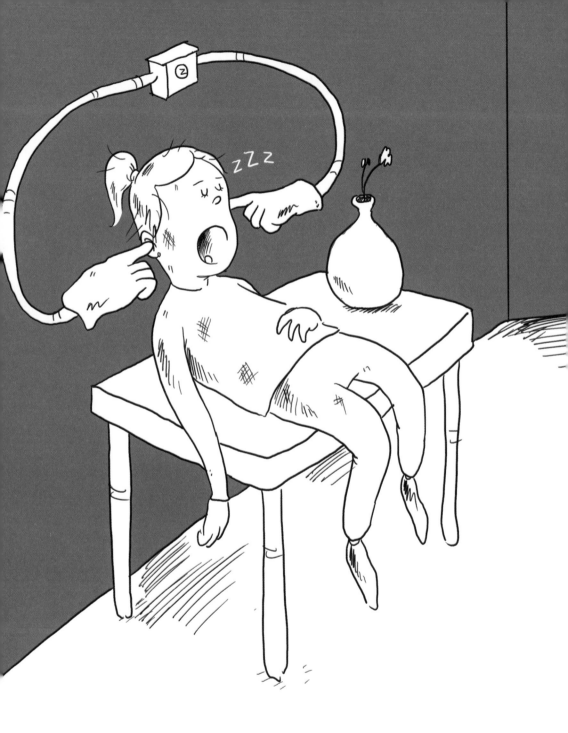

The screams turned to sobs,
The sobs slowed to moanin',
We sat on the couch
And watched DVR'd *Conan.*

I dozed off for a moment—
Or more, on reflection . . .
But don't tell the folks
Down at Child Protection.

The kid was not dropped,
The kid did not fall.
So no need to tell them—
Or the missus—at all.

I awoke to a show
That was not controversial.
Not *Conan,* but rather
Some lame infomercial.

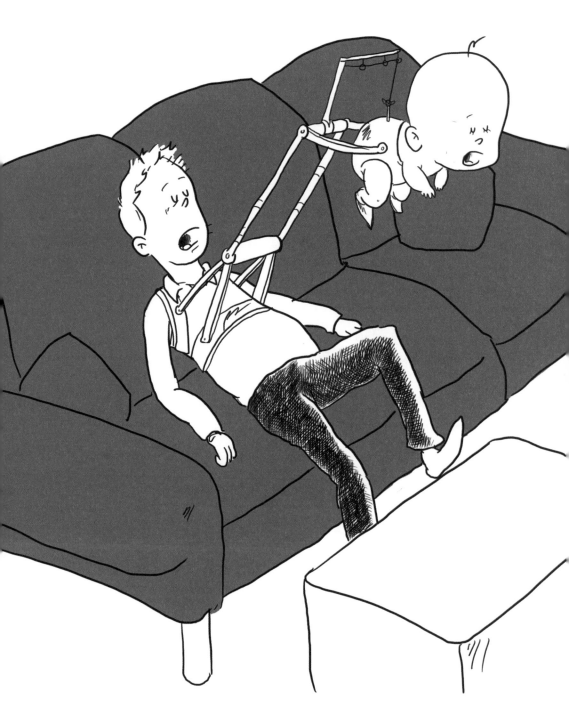

And when I woke up
I saw Baby was sleeping.
I slowly stood up
And then started my creeping.

I tiptoed to the stairs—
Which took, oh, two weeks.
I tried to avoid
The big step and its creaks.

It was 3:00 a.m. now,
Our home: still and quiet.
I placed her in the crib,
Which then started a riot.

She screamed at the instant
Her skin hit the mattress,
As if it were made
From, say, fire and cactus.

"Now, now," I said sweetly,
"Your mommy will take you."
To my wife I said only,
"Oh no—did she wake you?"

She took out the baby,
I slept like the dead.
'Round 4:30 or so,
My wife came back to bed.

And then five minutes later
(Perhaps it was ten),
You-know-who chose
To wake up once again.

Too soon to wake up,
Too late to re-doze.
We groaned out of bed,
And we pulled on our clothes.

We were like zombies:
I brushed with shampoo;
I may have used mouthwash
As aftershave, too.

She nursed the baby,
I nursed a sore head.
We both wished that we
Could climb back into bed.

We both felt exhausted,
Felt the old baby blues.
I headed for work,
And forgot to wear shoes.

So I turned right around
And went back in the house,
And that's when I saw
Spit-up on my wife's blouse.

My wife changed her top;
I slipped on my shoes.
For a moment, I dreamed of
A button called Snooze.

I buckled the car seat,
My wife fixed the strap,
When our bundle of joy
Made a bundle of crap.

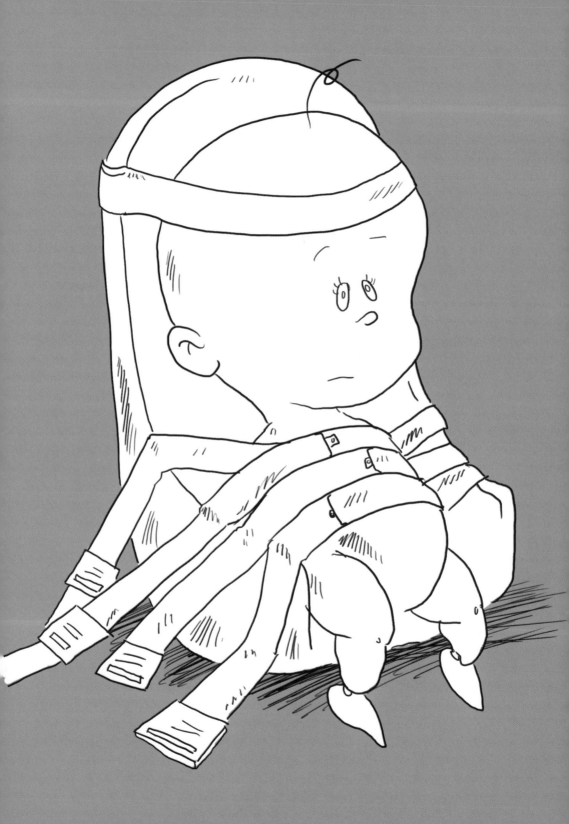

"Did she just go poopy?"
My wife asked, her eyes glassy.
"She did not," I pretended:
"I think she's just gassy."

The smell was just awful—
We tried not to hurl.
I turned on some music:
Katy's "I Kissed a Girl."

I thought I'd done well,
But my wife said, "No! No!
This song's not okay!
For our daughter!" and so,
She found some kids music
And turned up the sound,
And we learned how the wheels
On a bus go round, round.

I kept my eyes open,
But only just barely.
And now, baby was quiet,
Which happened so rarely.

We pulled into the day care,
And our luck changed a lot.
Right up in the front:
A free parking spot!

With the minivan parked,
I opened the doors.
I scooped up the baby,
Enjoying her snores.

Behind me, my wife
Closed *her* door with a boom—
But the baby stayed sleeping!
Good luck was in bloom.

We strode to the door
Of the day care in stride,
My wife pulled it open—
Or rather, she tried.

She pulled and she pulled,
And then she pulled some more.
But my lovable wife
Could not open the door.

I gave her the baby,
Who let out one cry.
I said, "If she wakes,
I think I'm gonna die."

Still the baby stayed sleeping,
Save for that single sob.
I calmly stepped forward
And reached for the knob.

Still that door wouldn't budge!
Was this some kind of trick?
Who would mess with us parents?
Only someone quite sick!

I said to my wife,
"Where is your iPhone, please?"
It was in her back pocket;
It slid out with ease.

I swiped to unlock it,
Then tried not to slam it
As I saw what I saw,
And then whispered "God *damn* it!"

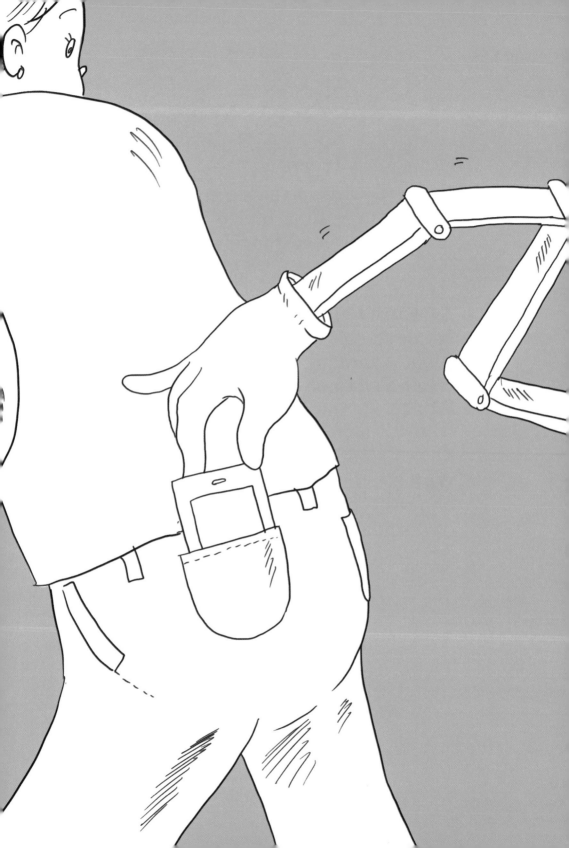

"What's wrong?" asked my wife,
"And why are you swearing?"
I took a deep breath,
And then started sharing.

"My dear," I said then,
"It was wrong that we came . . .
My dear,
What a shame!
What a shame!
What a shame!"

Then I showed her the phone
With the date on its screen.
She read "Saturday,"
And said: "I need caffeine."

We bundled the baby
Back into the car,
And headed for coffee
(I wished for a bar).

The baby stayed sleeping
For some time, I'd reckon—
By which I mean maybe
Two-thirds of one second.

Her screams went right on
Through the coffee drive-thru.
At one point, her mother
And I joined in, too.

We got to the house,
And we got her inside.
We both caffeinated;
And baby? She cried.

Too young for TV,
Too wound up for sleep . . .
Our kid needed something—
Ideally dirt cheap.

I again asked my wife
For her iPhone—while calm,
As it rang I just whispered,
"I'm calling your mom."

Soon her mother arrived,
And she said to us two,
"I'll take care of the baby.
Back to bed, both of you."

And my dear wife and I,
We knew just what to do.
We went back to bed.
That's what YOU would do, too!

The two of them played.
We lay there and cursed.
Napping while on a
Caffeine high's the worst.

ACKNOWLEDGMENTS

Thanks to Anya, Sierra, and Liam, for seemingly sharing at least some of my unabashed love for Dr. Seuss. And my incredibly patient wife, Lauren, read plenty of Seuss books to the kids in one room so that I could write this parody in another—thank you.

My agent, Rachel Sussman, calls me a "humorist," so I will forever be in love with her. Lara Asher at Lyons Press made this book a reality, which was an awfully nice thing of her to do.

Seth Brown helped me learn to rhyme better. Philip Michaels gave me my first paid writing gig. Jason Snell gave me permission to write this book. Oren Katzeff acknowledged me in his book.

Felix, your artwork is awesome. I owe a debt of gratitude to you, and to Reddit for leading me to you.

Quite frankly, a lot of good people are constantly very nice to me, which makes me both feel grateful and question their judgment. Thank you all.

Special, extra heartfelt thanks to Jake Rubin and Megan Morrison. They know what they did.

ABOUT THE AUTHORS

Lex Friedman is a grown-up with three kids and a wife, but he still clings to many of the same forms of entertainment that he loved as a kid. His love affair with Dr. Seuss books began early, and as a student at Brandeis University, he converted the school's student rulebook into Seussian metered rhyme for the campus humor magazine. He now writes news, reviews, tutorials, and opinion pieces for *Macworld* and Macworld.com; his website contributions are read millions of times each month. Friedman is the co-author of *The Snuggie Sutra,* which is as ridiculous as it sounds. He lives in New Jersey with his family. Find Lex on the web at lexfriedman.com and on Twitter as @lexfri.

Felix Schlater is a Virginia-based illustrator and graphic designer. When he's not drawing, he enjoys spending time with his wife and two crazy dogs.